Wha the World

by John Stewart
illustrated by Stephen Marchese

Harcourt
SCHOOL PUBLISHERS

Cover, ©Flip Nicklin/Minden Pictures; p.3, ©Kennan Ward/Corbis; p.4, ©Flip Nicklin/Minden Pictures; p.6(tr), ©Flip Nicklin/Minden Pictures; p.6(b), ©Armin Maywald/npl/Minden Pictures; p.9, ©James Gritz/Getty Images/PhotoDisc; p.10-11, ©Corel Stock Photo Library; p.12, ©Marc Bernardi/Alamy; p.13, Corel Stock Photo Library; p.14 Flip Nicklin/Minden Pictures.

Printed in China
ISBN 10: 0-15-351673-9
ISBN 13: 978-0-15-351673-3

Ordering Options
ISBN 10: 0-15-351215-6 (Grade 5 Advanced Collection)
ISBN 13: 978-0-15-351215-5 (Grade 5 Advanced Collection)
ISBN 10: 0-15-358156-5 (package of 5)
ISBN 13: 978-0-15-358156-4 (package of 5)

5 6 7 8 9 10   468   12 11 10 09

Whale-watching trips can be a mix of boredom and excitement. Watchers are much more likely to see waves than whales. However, the moment a whale pokes its head above a wave or a tail comes crashing down into the water, the hours of dutiful watching will seem worth it.

It's not hard to detect the amazing animals when they are nearby. Whales are huge and active, often doing fascinating things as they swim. Sometimes they *spy-hop,* resting vertically while popping their heads up above the water. At other times, they *lob-tail,* raising their massive tails into the air and bringing them down with a splat. They may also *breach,* or jump right out of the ocean.

Although whales might remind people of fish, they are really gigantic mammals. As mammals, they must breathe air into their lungs and therefore come to the surface from time to time. Instead of a nose with nostrils, a whale has a *blowhole* located on the top of its head. When a whale's blowhole appears above the water, a fountain of water may shoot high into the sky.

Like other mammals, whales give birth to live young. Different species have different gestation periods, ranging from ten to sixteen months. Only one baby whale, called a calf, is born at a time. Unlike human babies, the infant whale can move on its own immediately, so it is able to swim from the moment it is born. However, the calf depends on its mother for nourishment. The mother whale feeds her baby very rich milk. The milk's high fat content helps the baby stay warm in the cold waters that most whale species prefer.

Whales are mammals, so they are warm-blooded. That means they must maintain a normal body temperature. A few species live in rivers, but most of the world's whales inhabit the oceans. Many of these oceanic species thrive in the frigid waters that flow over the coldest parts of the earth. Unlike mammals on land, whales have no fur or hair to help keep them warm. Instead, they rely on *blubber,* which is a thick layer of fat right under their skin.

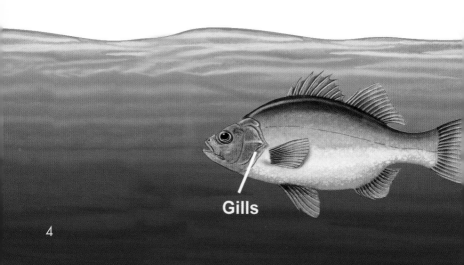

Gills

There are some easy ways to tell that a whale is a mammal, not a fish. Fish have gills, not lungs, and breathe underwater. If you see a blowhole, you're looking at a mammal. Also, a fish's tail stands vertically and moves side to side. A mammal's tail projects horizontally from the rear of its body and moves up and down.

The world's seventy-six species of whales are divided into two main groups—*baleen* whales and *toothed* whales. Surprisingly, most of the biggest whales are baleen whales—creatures without teeth. Baleen whales have baleen plates in their mouth that act as strainers. Baleen is a hard but elastic substance that grows in a comb-like structure hanging from the whale's upper jaw. The baleen contains hairy bristles. As the whale swims near the water's surface, it gulps huge amounts of water. Then the whale forces the water out of its mouth—through the baleen plates. Small food organisms get caught on the bristles, and the whale uses its tongue to guide them down its throat.

Dorsal Fin **Blowhole**
Flukes
Flipper

Almost 90% of whales fall into the toothed category. As you probably guessed, toothed whales have teeth. Most toothed whales are relatively small compared with baleen whales, but two kinds—killer whales and sperm whales—can grow quite large. Besides having teeth, toothed whales differ from baleen whales in another easily noticeable way. Baleen whales have two blowholes; toothed whales only have one.

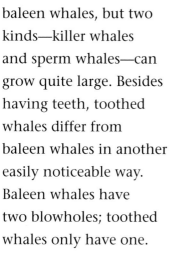

Toothed whale (at right) and baleen whale (below)

baleen

Here are some specific whale records:

- **Largest**
  The largest animal
  that has ever lived on
  earth is the blue whale. It can

  Blue Whale

  grow to around 90 to 100 feet (27–30 m)
  long and can weigh over 150 tons (136,078
  kg)! Blue whales are baleen whales.

- **Farthest-traveling**
  Gray whales, another
  species of baleen whale,
  migrate as far as 12,500 miles
  (20,117 km) each year. In the

  Gray Whale

  summer, they feed in the cold Arctic waters,
  but they give birth to their young each
  winter in the much warmer lagoons off Baja
  California. Gray whales swim fairly close to
  the coast, and thousands of people flock to
  America's Pacific shores to watch them travel
  in the spring and fall.

- **Deepest-diving**

  The champion diver in
  the whale world is the
  sperm whale, the largest of the
  toothed whales. Its favorite
  food is squid, which dwell down near the
  ocean floor. To get their tasty dinner, sperm
  whales regularly dive almost 4,000 feet
  (1,219 m) deep and can stay below for nearly
  two hours if they need to. The contents of
  one captured sperm whale's stomach revealed
  creatures that live almost 11,000 feet (3,353
  m) below the surface of the water!

  Sperm Whale

- **Longest tooth**

  The narwhal is a kind of
  toothed whale. All narwhals
  start out in life with two teeth
  approximately eight inches
  (20 cm) long in their upper jaws. When a
  male turns about a year old, however, its
  left tooth seems to spin out of control—
  literally. It grows longer and longer, spiraling
  clockwise out of the whale's mouth.
  Eventually, that tooth becomes a tusk that
  can extend as long as 10 feet (3.0 m)!

  Narwhal

8

Dolphins

Dolphins are toothed whales. A dolphin's sleek body allows it to swim at hunting speeds of up to 25 miles (40 km) per hour. When the dolphin is moving at a more relaxed pace—not exactly basking in the sun but peacefully swimming along—it still covers three to seven miles (4.8-11 km) in an hour.

There are thirty-seven species of dolphin in the world. Five of these species dwell in rivers in either Asia or South America. The rest make the ocean their home, and dolphins inhabit the seas of almost every region of the earth.

Most dolphin species have long snouts that look similar to a bird's beak. One dolphin species that does not have the beaklike feature but does have a huge mouth full of sharp teeth  is the killer whale. Killer whales can be found all over the globe. They, like other dolphins, have become popular in aquariums, theme parks, and even in the movies.

A good reason for the dolphin's popularity is its intelligence. These smart creatures can solve problems requiring a great deal of thought. In the wild, they communicate with one another to cooperate in hunting and other day-to-day tasks. Scientists rank dolphins, along with primates, as the most intelligent animals on earth.

Since a dolphin is a mammal, it is vital for it to breathe air. Therefore, like other members of the whale family, a dolphin comes equipped with a blowhole on the top of its head. It is breathtaking to watch dolphins as they leap out of the water, arcing beautifully above the surface. They exhale with a short burst from their blowhole and then take a long breath.

Be careful not to confuse whales' blowholes with the noses of other mammals. Blowholes are employed only in breathing, not as organs to pick up smells. In fact, dolphins do not have a sense of smell that they can use to hunt, but they compensate by having excellent eyesight and amazing hearing in most cases.

Dolphins travel in groups and are extremely social. They maintain contact with one another by making whistling and clicking sounds. They communicate often and for a variety of reasons. Sometimes they just want to exchange greetings, but dolphin communications are usually about more important matters. They warn one another of possible underwater dangers and also share information about the location of food. Dolphins work together to capture their prey and to fend off any potentially damaging creatures.

Dolphin clicks, which are emitted from a mechanism just below their blowholes, may not sound like much to human ears. Amazingly, though, these clicks are actually a natural form of sonar, which is like underwater radar. The clicks bounce off nearby objects, sending echoes back through the water. These echoes are picked up by dolphins through their teeth and nerves in their bottom jaws, and the information gets processed in their brains. The dolphins can then "see" an image based on sound, not sight. Dolphins' ability to use "echolocation" to pinpoint food helps them survive in even the murkiest of waters.

Dolphins

People often make the mistake of referring to dolphins as "porpoises." Actually, dolphins and porpoises are two entirely different groups of toothed whales. Although most dolphins have beaks, none of the six species of porpoises does. If you were analyzing the differences between these two creatures, you would see that a dolphin's teeth are pointed, while a porpoise's are shaped like shovels. Their behaviors are different as well. Porpoises travel in very small groups, from two to four. They are also not as sociable with each other as many dolphin species are.

Unfortunately, whales are creatures that may be facing the threat of extinction. Many whale species are already endangered, and others are likely to become threatened if humans do not do something to protect them and their environment. The world would be far different without these magnificent giants of the deep.

Think Critically

1. How can you distinguish dolphins from porpoises?

2. Dolphins have a natural sonar system that helps them navigate and locate prey. Explain how it works.

3. Compare and contrast baleen whales and toothed whales.

4. What is the author's purpose for writing this book?

5. Of all the animals described in this book, which is your favorite? Explain your answer.

 Science

Another Whale Use the Internet or other library resources to learn more about another whale that has not been described in this book. Illustrate and summarize your findings on a poster.

School-Home Connection Summarize this book for your family. Invite them to talk about the differences between whales and fish. Encourage them to tell what they find most interesting about the differences.

Word Count: 1,547